ES

ETICS

CORGI BOOKS

THE GOLDEN RULES OF ATHLETICS

A CORGI BOOK 0 552 12597 0

First publication in Great Britain

PRINTING HISTORY
Corgi edition published 1985

Corgi Books are published by Transworld Publishers Ltd.,
Century House, 61-63 Uxbridge Road, Ealing, London W5 5SA,
in Australia by Transworld Publishers (Aust.) Pty. Ltd.,
26 Harley Crescent, Condell Park, NSW 2200, and in New
Zealand by Transworld Publishers (N.Z.) Ltd., Cnr. Moselle
and Waipareira Avenues, Henderson, Auckland.

Made and printed in Great Britain by
Hunt Barnard Printing Ltd., Aylesbury, Bucks.

Races are started by the report of a pistol or similar apparatus, fired upward into the air.

Be extremely careful when carrying equipment, especially the javelin, shot or hammer, to and from a meeting.

Once the high-jump has commenced the competitor may not receive any help or advice from anyone.

In the high-jump wait until your number or name is called before commencing to jump.

The hammer must land within the inner edge of the sector lines.

Throwing the hammer is difficult for the beginner
and much practise and advice will be needed.

In the 4 x 400m relay, baton passing must be practised and perfected if a team is to have any chance of
winning.

The baton in the relay race must be handed to an official at the end of the race.

Kit should be chosen to suit the weather conditions.

Try to keep as dry and as warm as possible before and during your event.

Shot putting should be practised in designated areas only.

In the marathon, sponging points are provided, supplying water only.

Support for the spine and back muscles is allowed in the discus.

Competitors in any event must abide by the decision of a judge, marshal or any other official.

In the hammer event the competitor must not leave the circle until the hammer has landed.

The competitor in the high-jump should warm up thoroughly prior to his or her jump.

When putting the shot, the shot must be 'pushed' rather than 'thrown' or any other method.

A steeplechaser will be disqualified if he fails to go over or through the water at the water jump.

During the 50km race walking competition the walker will aim for approximately 1100 strides per km.

47,321........
47,322........
47,323......
47,324....

In the race walking Judges are appointed to see that unbroken contact with the ground is maintained.

In the pole-vault a competitor may not move the position of his hands after leaving the ground.

Cross-country races are marked by flags and arrows which have to be closely followed.

**Starting blocks must be constructed entirely of rigid
materials and must be securely fixed to the ground.**

A failure is counted in the long-jump if the competitor fails to land within the landing area.

If the judges and track officials decide that a meeting or an event must take place, then all competitors must abide by the ruling.

A competitor should not remain in the arena after his or her event has been completed.

If the following wind is blowing at more than 2 metres per second in hurdle or sprint events, then any record time cannot be ratified.

Competitors may run barefoot but remember it can be dangerous.

In the pole-vault event the length of the run-up is unlimited.

A hurdler will be disqualified if he jumps any hurdle not in his or her own lane.

The javelin must not be thrown unless the marshal has given the all clear.

The athlete must be completely fit to compete in his or her event.

A competitor in a track event finishes when his or her torso touches the tape. This does not include the arms, legs or head.

A high-jump is counted a failure if the competitor knocks the bar off the supports.

Should a competitor wish to protest about the actions of another competitor, he should contact the track referee and not endeavour to resolve it himself.

The athlete should be sensible in regards to his intake of fluid prior to a competition, as too much fluid, especially fizzy drinks, could have dire consequences.

To feel comfortable during hurdling, the competitor should wear loose-fitting clothing.

If possible, try out any athletics equipment before
buying it.

Track competitors will be disqualified for receiving any assistance from persons within the arena.

In the hammer, discus or shot event a competitor may use his own implement but it must be inspected and approved by the referee.

42

The pole-vault can be a dangerous event and therefore the technique of the competitor has to be practised and perfected.

In the hurdle, the trailing of a leg around the side of a
hurdle is not permissible.

Always wear comfortable footwear when running.

If you do not win your race or event, be sporting about congratulating the winner.

Above all else, athletics is to be enjoyed . . .